ALTERNATOR BOOKS™

ELECTRICITY INVESTIGATIONS

KATIE MARSICO

To the administrators, teachers, staff, and students at
Edison Elementary School in Elmhurst, Illinois

Content consultant: Kevin Finerghty, adjunct professor of Geology at State University of New York, Oswego; Earth science teacher at Pulaski Academy and Central Schools, Pulaski, New York

Lerner Publications Company
A division of Lerner Publishing Group, Inc.
241 First Avenue North
Minneapolis, MN 55401 USA

For reading levels and more information, look up this title at www.lernerbooks.com.

Main body text set in Aptifer Slab Regular 11.5/18.
Typeface provided by Linotype AG.

Library of Congress Cataloging-in-Publication Data

Names: Marsico, Katie, 1980–
Title: Electricity investigations / by Katie Marsico.
Description: Minneapolis: Lerner Publications, [2017] | Series: Key questions in physical science | Audience: Age 8–12. | Audience: Grade 4 to 6. | Includes bibliographical references and index.
Identifiers: LCCN 2016041002 (print) | LCCN 2016044082 (ebook) | ISBN 9781512440072 (lb : alk. paper) | ISBN 9781512449556 (eb pdf)
Subjects: LCSH: Electricity—Juvenile literature.
Classification: LCC QC527.2 .M3554 2017 (print) | LCC QC527.2 (ebook) | DDC 537—dc23

LC record available at https://lccn.loc.gov/2016041002

Manufactured in the United States of America
1-42269-26126-1/16/2017

CONTENTS

HOW COULD SCIENTISTS LIGHT UP A CITY?

It's September 4, 1882. You're strolling through New York City when you notice a huge crowd on Pearl Street. Suddenly, at three o'clock in the afternoon, you see a flash. For the first time ever, roughly four hundred electric lamps are shining on Pearl Street.

Modern people depend on electricity to operate everything from televisions to trains. Electricity is a form of **energy**. We also rely on electricity to heat and cool buildings and, of course, to provide light.

Yet this wasn't always the case. It took scientists a long time and a lot of testing to bring electricity to Pearl Street—and beyond! At first, people didn't know what electricity was. Still, they noticed its effects on the world around them. They mainly **observed** how a strange force caused certain objects to be attracted to each other.

Scientists asked themselves questions about this force. After they finally identified it as electricity, they had even more questions! They wondered how electricity reacted with

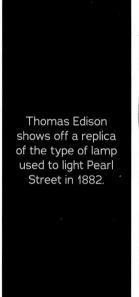

Thomas Edison shows off a replica of the type of lamp used to light Pearl Street in 1882.

other forces, such as magnetism. They also wanted to know if and how electricity could be used to do work.

Like detectives, scientists searched for clues to investigate such mysteries. During their investigations, they conducted many exciting experiments. These tests helped them collect data, or information. After reviewing their data, scientists formed conclusions, or answers to their questions. Finally, they shared what they had discovered.

This is called scientific inquiry. It's what allowed US inventor Thomas Edison to light up Pearl Street in 1882. Like many scientists before and after him, Edison changed the world by investigating electricity!

CHAPTER 1

WHAT IS ELECTRICITY?

If you didn't have electricity, how would you play video games or charge a cell phone? You probably find it hard to imagine life without electricity. But what exactly is electricity?

One way to answer this question is to think about what electricity does. As energy, it travels through wires and helps operate machines. Scientists also explain electricity by describing what it's made from—a flow of electrical charges. A charge is a property of **matter**.

Electrical charges flow from an energy source through wires to power devices and machines.

Some charges are negative, and others are positive. Opposite charges attract. Similar charges **repel** each other. People noticed the effects of opposite electrical charges as early as 600 BCE. The ancient Greeks were amazed by how feathers stuck to amber after they rubbed it with animal fur. Rubbing this mineral gave it a negative electrical charge. In turn, the amber attracted objects with a positive charge.

The Greeks didn't know it, but they were observing static electricity. Static electricity is energy that builds up in one spot. It's one of two main forms of electricity. The other is current electricity. That's energy that travels from place to place in a flow, or current.

In the eighteenth century, Benjamin Franklin wondered whether people could harness the energy from lightning.

A CLOSER LOOK AT LIGHTNING

Centuries later, scientists were determined to understand electricity better. They searched for clues in the world around them.

CAN SCIENTISTS CONTROL LIGHTNING?

A lightning rod is a metal rod or wire attached to a tall building and to the ground. Benjamin Franklin designed lightning rods to prevent lightning from damaging buildings. When lightning strikes a building, it can cause fires or power surges. By providing a path for the lightning, the rod directs electrical energy into the ground instead.

Lightning strikes the rod on top of One World Trade Center in New York City.

THE CHARGES THAT MAKE UP LIGHTNING

Static electricity builds up in storm clouds. Eventually, a lightning bolt transports an electrical current from clouds to the ground.

For example, Benjamin Franklin suspected lightning was a form of electrical energy. Legend has it that Franklin saw an opportunity to investigate his idea during a thunderstorm in Philadelphia, Pennsylvania, in 1752.

How could Franklin test lightning for an electrical charge? The story says he flew a kite attached to a metal key during the thunderstorm. He knew that metal carried an electrical charge. So he predicted it would attract any electrical energy in the lightning bolt. Franklin also believed that the kite string would serve as a conductor, a

We don't know for sure whether Franklin really performed the famous kite experiment. Testing electrical currents in a lightning storm could have harmed or even killed him.

material that an electrical current passes through.

Franklin used a wire to connect the key to a glass jar coated with metal. When lightning struck Franklin's kite, sparks moved down the string and the wire and into the jar. His experiment showed that lightning began as static electricity that built up in a storm cloud. Eventually, it became current electricity and traveled to objects on the ground.

CHAPTER 2

HOW ARE CURRENTS CREATED?

Where else does electricity come from? In the 1780s, Luigi Galvani wondered whether frog muscles could produce electricity. Galvani used metal hooks to hold a dead frog's legs in place. When he touched a leg—and hook—with a metal **probe**, the leg moved! Galvani concluded that animal muscles were a source of electrical energy.

Alessandro Volta disagreed. Volta believed that what Galvani saw was the result of contact between the metal hook and probe.

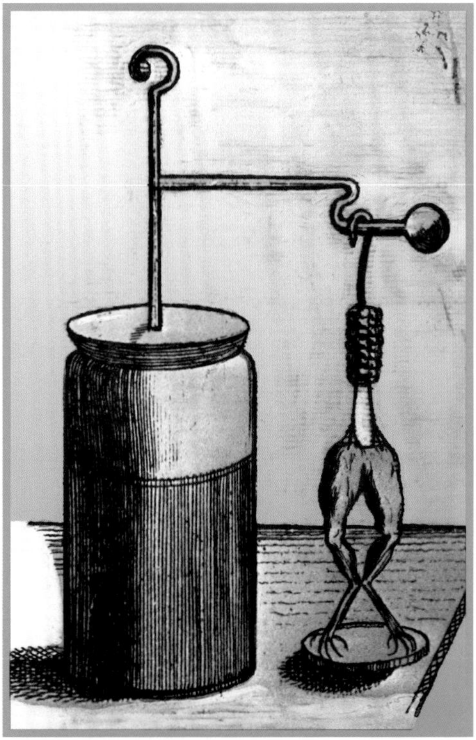

Galvani's wife was preparing a frog for dinner when he bumped it with a metal tool. The frog moved!

SCIENCE IN PRACTICE

Volta designed an experiment involving two metals—zinc and silver. He wanted to see if they reacted in a way that produced an electrical current. So he created a pile of **alternating** zinc and silver discs. Between the discs, Volta inserted strips of cloth soaked in chemicals that help conduct electricity. Finally, he connected wire to either end of the pile *(below)*. Ultimately, Volta's pile *did* generate a current—and became the first electric battery!

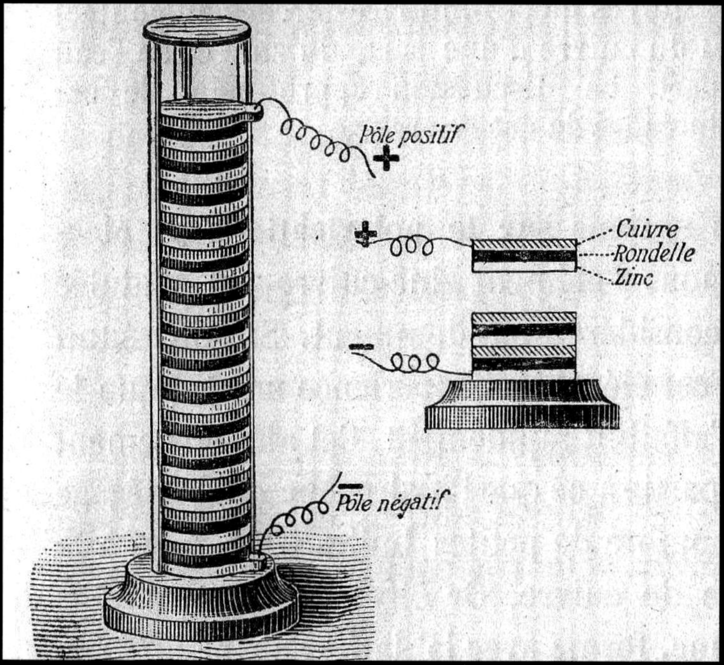

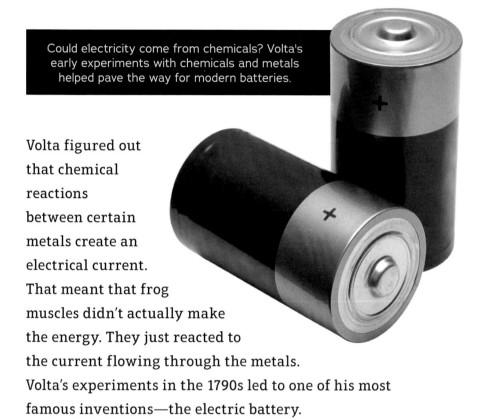

Could electricity come from chemicals? Volta's early experiments with chemicals and metals helped pave the way for modern batteries.

Volta figured out that chemical reactions between certain metals create an electrical current. That meant that frog muscles didn't actually make the energy. They just reacted to the current flowing through the metals. Volta's experiments in the 1790s led to one of his most famous inventions—the electric battery.

Batteries use chemical reactions to create electricity. They are still an important power source, especially in devices such as flashlights or watches.

FIGURING OUT HOW FORCES ARE LINKED

Chemical reactions aren't the only way to generate electricity. In 1820 Hans Christian Ørsted was demonstrating how to heat wire with an electrical current. He had placed a compass nearby to conduct a separate experiment on magnetism. Ørsted knew magnetism is the force that causes certain metals to be attracted to each other. What he didn't know was why the nearby compass needle moved when he began flowing an electrical current. How were magnetism and electricity linked?

André-Marie Ampère tried to solve this mystery. Ampère's experiments in 1820 involved flowing electrical currents in the same direction through **parallel** wires. He discovered that the wires attracted each other. When he made the currents flow in opposite directions, the wires repelled each other. Ampère concluded that when the wires carried electricity, they acted like magnets.

The ampere (amp for short), a unit of measurement for electricity, is named after Ampère.

AMPÈRE'S WIRES: ELECTROMAGNETISM

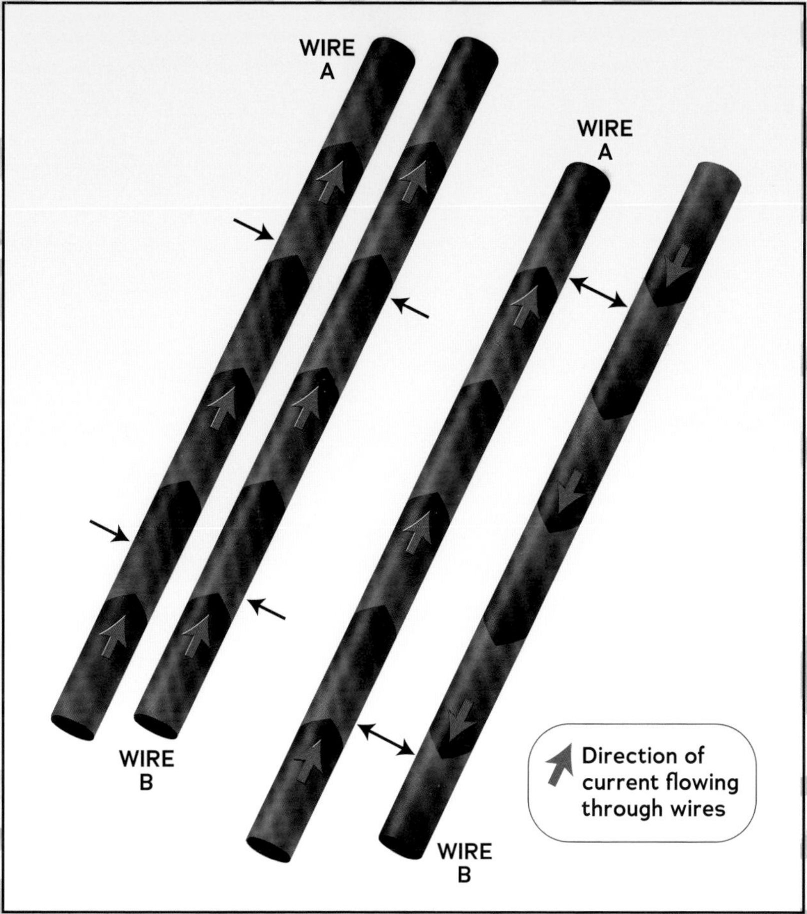

When the currents in two parallel wires flow in the same direction (*left*), the wires attract each other. When the currents flow in opposite directions (*right*), the wires repel each other.

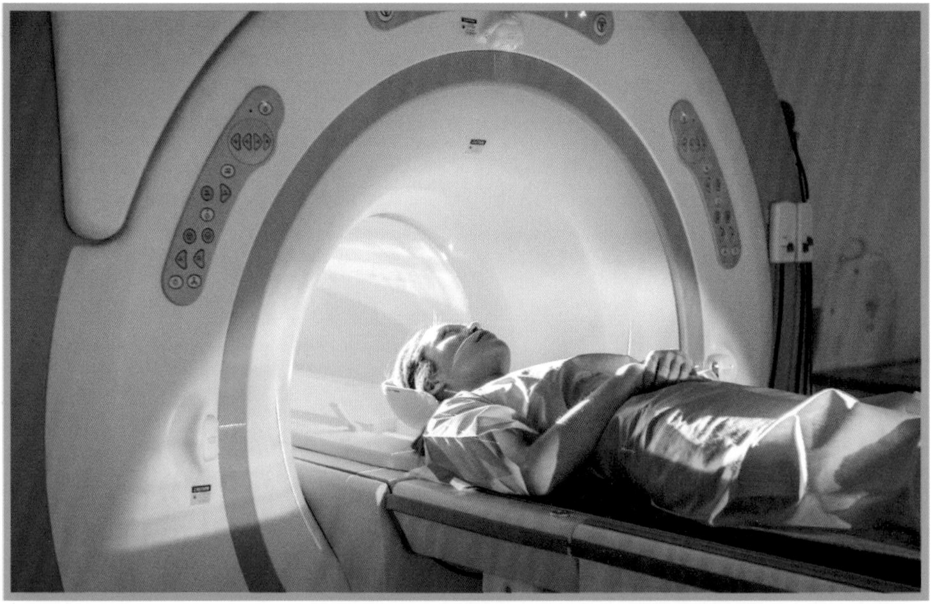

Magnetic resonance imaging (MRI) uses electromagnetism to take pictures of what's under a person's skin.

Ampère named the relationship between electricity and magnetism "electrodynamics." It is also known as electromagnetism.

Michael Faraday later built on Ampère's conclusion. In 1830 Faraday discovered electromagnetic induction—using a magnetic field to generate electricity!

CHAPTER 3

HOW DOES ELECTRICITY TRAVEL?

These days, electricity is distributed, or spread, throughout your entire community. Yet before 1882, this may not have seemed possible. As Edison continued to experiment with electricity, he faced a problem. How could Edison **illuminate** an entire town? He used battery power

It may seem easy to flip a light switch, but scientists spent centuries asking questions and testing ideas to make your lights safe and functional.

to light wires inside bulbs at his laboratory. But batteries supplied a limited amount of electricity. Edison needed a steady power source that would produce an ongoing electrical current.

Edison decided to build a generator. This machine turns one form of energy into another. Edison's generator operated using electromagnetic induction. A steam engine moved wire **coils** between a pair of huge magnets to create an electrical current.

This 1879 lamp was one step in Edison's process of figuring out how to power lightbulbs with electrical currents.

Edison's generator produced a direct current (DC). This meant that electricity flowed in only one direction. Edison was able to use DC to amaze the crowds on Pearl Street. But delivering power greater distances was harder. For starters, it wasn't easy to increase the voltage, or force, of DC. Yet high voltages were necessary for currents to travel farther. To make DC work, Edison had to build a power station every few miles.

HOW COULD ELECTRICITY TRAVEL FARTHER?

Nikola Tesla was convinced there was a better way to distribute electricity. In Tesla's opinion, it didn't make sense to keep building power stations to support DC.

Nikola Tesla didn't think Edison's DC distribution was very efficient. But he had to work hard to get people to try his alternating current (AC) idea.

SCIENCE IN PRACTICE

While experimenting, Tesla observed how AC caused a magnetic field to rotate, or turn. Tesla wondered what would happen if he reversed this process. Would a rotating magnetic field generate AC? He proved it would! In the late 1880s, he used this knowledge to develop an induction motor. It ran on electromagnetic energy.

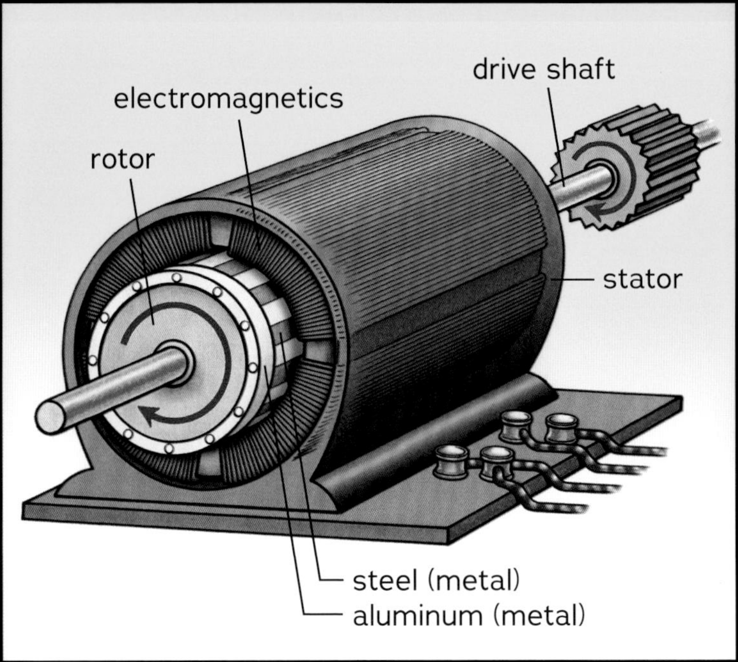

In an induction motor, rotating magnetic fields in parts called the rotor and the stator cause attraction and repulsion. This makes the rotor turn.

A battery powers the electric Nissan Leaf. An AC charger is the standard way to recharge the battery, but some models have a DC option for quicker charging.

Instead, he suggested generating currents that would alternate direction several times per second. It was easier to increase or decrease the voltage of these alternating currents (AC). Starting in the 1890s, Tesla's AC made it possible to distribute electricity longer distances.

Modern AC brings electricity to homes and businesses. AC also powers most modern appliances. Yet people still depend on DC to operate devices ranging from LED displays to electric cars. DC power tends to be more common in devices that run on lower voltages.

CHAPTER 4

HOW DOES POWER GET TO YOUR LIGHT SWITCH?

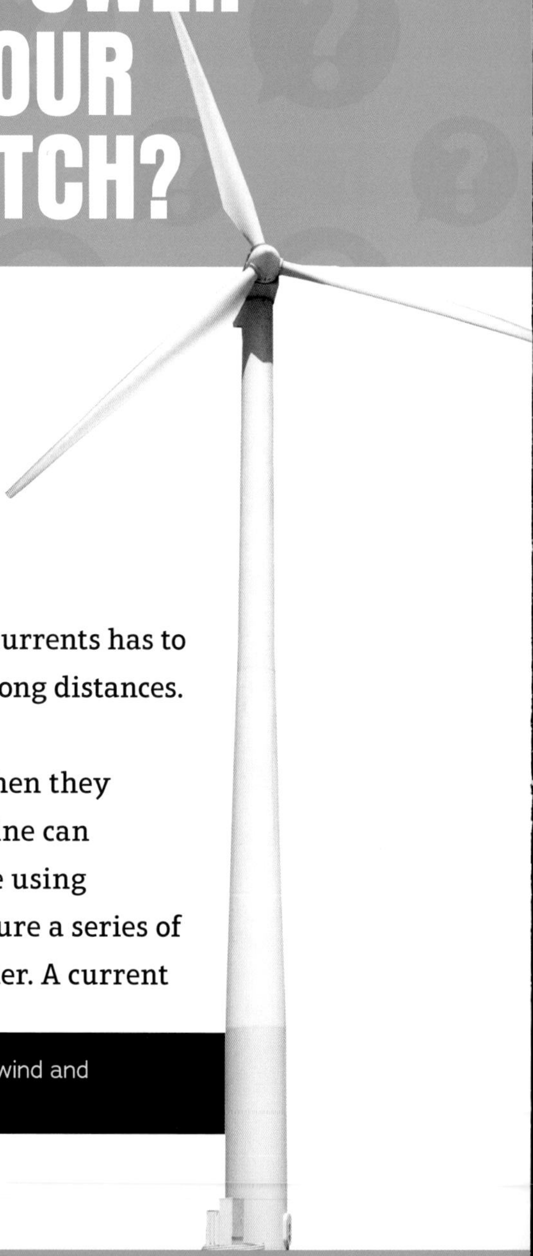

Let's take a look at how electricity gets from a power plant to a switch in your home! Scientists use coal, gas, water, and wind to run the generators in power plants. Once the generators produce electricity, the voltage of the currents has to be increased to help the power travel long distances. How is that possible?

Scientists discovered the answer when they invented the transformer. This machine can increase or decrease electrical voltage using electromagnetism. Transformers feature a series of wire coils wound around a metal center. A current

Wind turbines harness the energy from wind and send it to power plants.

leaving a power plant passes through several coils as it flows into a transformer. When it flows out of the transformer, it passes through even more coils. Changing the number of coils changes the electromagnetism surrounding the current. Increasing the number of coils steps up the current's voltage.

Transformers ensure that the currents leaving a power plant are strong enough to travel long distances. But sometimes electrical currents can be *too* strong. Extremely high voltages can damage wires and appliances within your home. They can also cause **electrical shock**. So scientists have set up transformers along power lines.

Power plants have changed a lot since the nineteenth century, when Edison first lit up Pearl Street.

When an outgoing current passes through a decreased number of coils, its voltage is decreased. Transformers get electricity where it needs to go—and they make sure it's safe to use once it gets there!

WHAT HAPPENS IN YOUR HOME?

Once voltage is decreased, an electrical current travels from outdoor power lines into your home. An electrical line called a service drop links a utility pole directly to your home or building. The current then moves through

When Edison began distributing DC electricity in the nineteenth century, he had to build power stations every few miles. Modern power lines and AC can deliver electricity from a power plant all the way to your home!

a meter. This device tracks how much electricity your family uses.

How does electricity flow to all the different parts of your home? Scientists have developed a kind of electrical map. This map starts with the service panel. Here the current is divided into circuits. These are closed paths that distribute electricity throughout a building.

Of course, scientists want people to use electricity safely. That means preventing too much electrical current from passing through your home's wires. Transformers are one tool used for this. So are fuses and breakers, devices that stop wires from becoming overloaded.

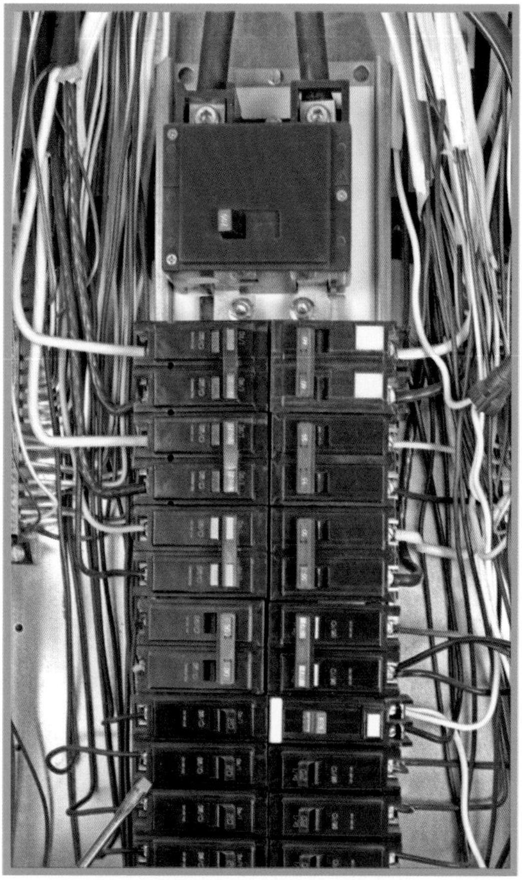

A breaker box regulates the voltage that travels from a service panel to appliances. If too much current goes through the wires, a breaker stops the current from flowing.

How does the electricity in these wires finally reach lights and other electric appliances in your home? Scientists have developed technology such as switches, plugs, and outlets. You access electrical power in your home's wiring when you flip switches or connect plugs to outlets. Would you have guessed that this whole process is at play whenever you turn on a light?

The toggle light switch was invented in 1917. Before then a person had to turn a key on a lamp to light up a room.

Scientists have spent centuries asking questions and exploring possibilities. Their investigations have brought people a long way since Pearl Street. Perhaps one day *you'll* be involved in an electricity investigation that changes the world!

FROM POWER PLANT TO LIGHT SWITCH

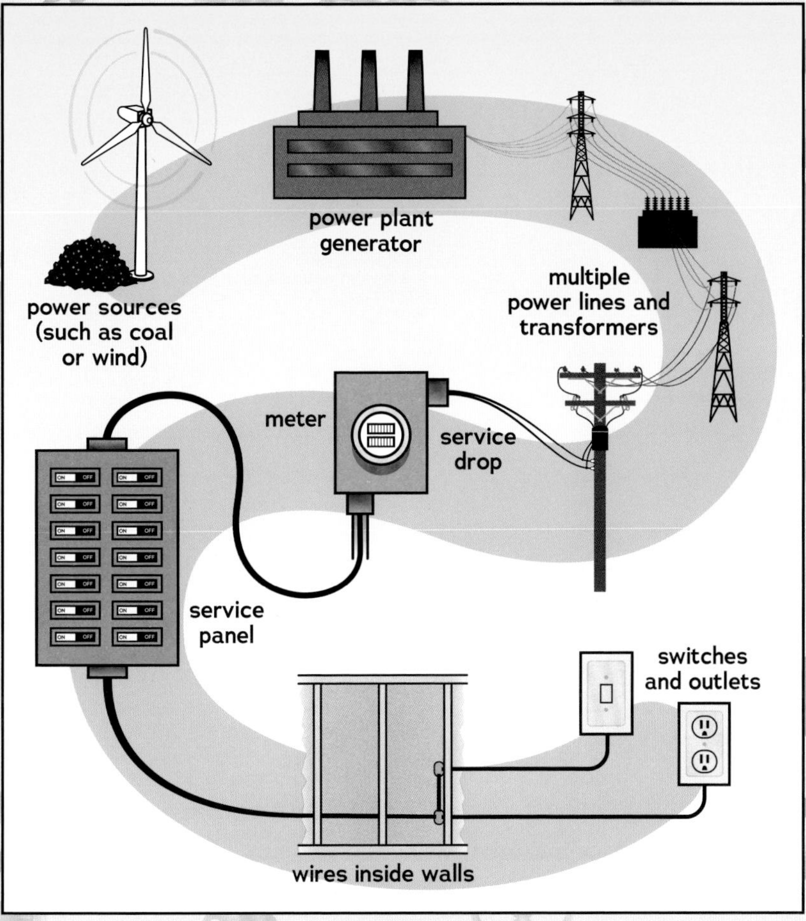

Countless scientists and engineers have worked on the parts that make up our modern system of electricity. What questions would you ask to improve this system?

TRY IT!

Circuits help distribute electricity throughout your home. A resistor in a circuit limits how much current flows through wiring. It prevents damage from overload. Any appliance on a circuit acts as a resistor.

But why do some resistors work better than others? Do certain features such as length affect the flow of electrical current? Let's find out! Use pencils to create your own resistors. Safety is important to any scientific investigation. Be sure an adult helps you!

WHAT YOU'LL NEED

- three AA batteries
- a AA battery holder
- three alligator clip leads (red, black, and green)
- a mini lightbulb screw base
- a screwdriver (possibly)
- a mini lightbulb
- a ruler
- a hacksaw
- six No. 2 pencils
- a sheet of paper
- a pencil sharpener

WHAT YOU'LL DO

- Put the three AA batteries in your battery holder. Be sure to line up the positive (+) symbols on the batteries with the + symbols in the holder.
- Check the holder and locate the exposed red wire coming out of it. Connect this wire to your red alligator clip lead. (Red wiring is often used in positive connections.)
- Next, connect the exposed black wire to your black clip. (Black wiring is often used in negative connections.)
- Attach the other end of the black clip to a screw on your mini lightbulb screw base. (Your adult helper might need to use a screwdriver to loosen the screw.)
- Screw your mini lightbulb into the base.
- Attach one end of the green clip to a screw on the base.

- You've created a circuit! Get ready to test it. Touch the exposed ends of your red and green clips together. If your circuit works, your bulb should light up. If it doesn't, be sure the bulb is tightly screwed into the base. Also check your batteries and clip connections. The circuit may not work properly if your batteries are backward or your connections are loose.
- Have your adult helper use the ruler and hacksaw to cut your No. 2 pencils. Trim the pencils to the following lengths: 1.5 inches (3.8 centimeters), 3 inches (7.6 cm), 4.5 inches (11 cm), and 6 inches (15 cm).
- Divide the sheet of paper into two columns. Label the first column "Pencil Length." Label the second column "Brightness of Bulb." In the first line of the first column, write "0 inches."
- Sharpen both ends of each pencil. Use your ruler to measure the tip-to-tip lengths. Record them in the first column.
- Start by studying the brightness of your bulb without a resistor. This involves touching the exposed metal tips of your red and green clips together without a pencil. Use a "0 to 5" scale to measure brightness, with 0 equal to no light and 5 equal to extremely bright light. Record your observation in the second column.
- Test all your pencil resistors. Connect each one to your circuit with the red and green clips. Then record how brightly the bulb shines!

FOLLOW UP

Review your results. Use the following questions to form conclusions about what your experiment proves. Write your conclusions on the back of your chart.

- How did the brightness of the bulb change as the lengths of your pencil resistors changed?
- How does the length of a resistor affect resistance?
- How does resistance affect the amount of current moving through a circuit?

GLOSSARY

alternating: taking turns

coils: lengths of wire wound into circles or spirals

electrical shock: a sudden and often dangerous discharge of electricity through part of the body

energy: usable power or the ability to do work

illuminate: light up

matter: anything that has mass, takes up space, and is part of the physical world

observed: watched carefully, with attention to details

parallel: side by side and the same distance apart

probe: a slender, blunt-ended surgical instrument

repel: push back or away

FURTHER INFORMATION

Alliant Energy Kids—All about Electricity
http://www.alliantenergykids.com/EnergyBasics/AllAboutElectricity

Christensen, Victoria G. *How Batteries Work*. Minneapolis: Lerner Publications, 2017.

Energy Kids: Electricity
http://www.eia.gov/kids/energy.cfm?page=electricity_home-basics

Explain That Stuff!—Electricity
http://www.explainthatstuff.com/electricity.html

Hayes, Amy. *Freaky Stories about Electricity.* New York: Gareth Stevens, 2017.

Kids' Corner: What Is Electricity?
http://kids.saveonenergy.ca/en/what-is-electricity

Marsico, Katie. *Key Discoveries in Physical Science.* Minneapolis: Lerner Publications, 2015.

Polinsky, Paige V. *Super Simple Experiments with Electricity: Fun and Innovative Science Projects*. Minneapolis: Abdo, 2017.

Roland, James. *How Circuits Work*. Minneapolis: Lerner Publications, 2017.

INDEX

PHOTO ACKNOWLEDGMENTS

The images in this book are used with the permission of: © iStockphoto.com/kotoffei (background science items); © iDesign/Shutterstock.com (background—question mark); © Bettmann Archive/Getty Images, p. 5; © Vasilius/Shutterstock.com, p. 6; Library of Congress (LC-USZ61-1317), p. 7; © iStockphoto.com/CribbVisuals, p. 8; © Laura Westlund/Independent Picture Service, pp. 9, 15, 20, 27; © ClassicStock/Alamy, p. 10; © Bettmann Archive/Getty Images, p. 11; © rakim/iStock/Thinkstock, p. 12; © Gillard/Wikimedia Commons (public domain), p. 13; © DeAgostini/Getty Images, p. 14; © Monty Rakusen/Cultura RF/Getty Images, p. 16; © Warren Diggles/Alamy, p. 17; © SSPL/Getty Images, p. 18; © Everett Collection Inc/Alamy, p. 19; © Todd Bannor/Alamy, p. 21; © iStockphoto.com/globestock, p. 22; © Zoonar GmbH/Alamy, p. 23; © iStockphoto.com/iliffd, p. 24; © Don Nichols/Getty Images, p. 25; © iStockphoto.com/michaelmjc, p. 26.

Cover: © iStockphoto.com/tolokonov (lightning); © iStockphoto.com/kotoffei (background science items); © iDesign/Shutterstock.com (background—question mark).